T0081977

Captain Noah
and his Floating Zoo

BY MICHAEL FLANDERS & JOSEPH HOROVITZ

Cantata in popular style for unison or
two-part voices & piano, with
optional bass & drums

NOVELLO PUBLISHING LIMITED

Order No: NOV 200135

PREFACE

We chose Noah as our subject because it offered such a splendid, dramatic shape for setting to music as a group of songs. If you look it up, you will see that our version follows the Old Testament story very closely (when we did, we were surprised to find we had forgotten all about the Raven and the domestication of animals!). The work is not intended as a contribution to 'pop' religion. We hope it will be useful wherever and whenever groups of singers and musicians need a work of some length to perform together, and that they will arrange, divide and adapt it (within reason) as best suits their available talent and the occasion. It has been designed as a choral, rather than a theatrical, piece; but various semi-dramatic effects or stagings may suggest themselves.

The work can be performed with piano accompaniment alone, but a separate part each for string bass and jazz drums is available on hire. Guitar may be added, playing from the score. Various optional percussion instruments may be used here and there for special effects, such as at the start (thunder) and in No. 3 where maracas, claves and tambourines may help to accentuate the Latin-American flavour of the Samba.

The printed suggestions in the vocal parts ('solo', 'all', 'some' and 'others' etc.) may be helpful when distributing sections among larger groups, especially in schools. Where the vocal line divides into two (occasionally into three), we suggest a simple division of singers into high-voice and low-voice groups, irrespective of sex.

Finally, we strongly recommend our metronome markings, and we do feel that the piece should be performed as a continuous whole, with the shortest possible breaks between each number.

Michael Flanders & Joseph Horovitz

Duration (approx.) 26 minutes

Permission to give stage performances of this work should be obtained from the publisher. A performing fee will be charged, based on the price of admission and the size of the auditorium. When no charge for admission is made, the performing fee will only be nominal.

Permission to give concert performances must be obtained from The Performing Right Society Limited, 29/33 Berners Street, London W1P 4AA or its affiliates unless the owner or occupier of the premises being used holds a licence from the Society.

No part of this publication may be copied or reproduced in any form or by any means without the prior permission of Novello & Company Limited.

CAPTAIN NOAH AND HIS FLOATING ZOO

Cantata in popular style for unison or two-part voices and piano,
with optional bass and drums
by
MICHAEL FLANDERS and JOSEPH HOROVITZ

Introduction

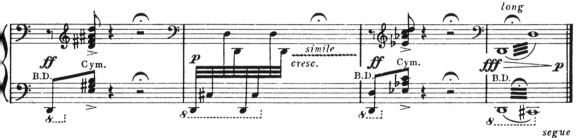

No. 1

19888

© Novello & Company Limited 1970

should have been good what I made but it turned out bad. There's

no-thing but sin-ning, wick-ed-ness and vi-o-lence there! Re-

mind me to wash man-kind right out of my hair!

I'm gon-na make it rain and rain and rain and

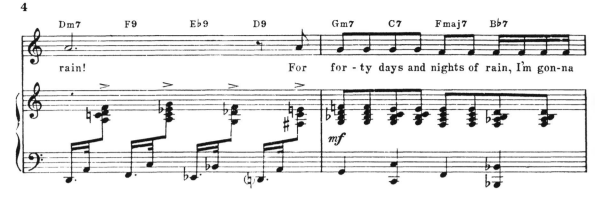

rain! For for - ty days and nights of rain, I'm gon-na

wash those sin-ners down the drain! Rain and rain and rain and rain and

rain! But

No - ah and his fam-i - ly they've been good. Go,

No-ah, build me an ark, of go-pher-wood; make it

four-fif-ty long, by se-ven-ty-five feet wide, and

three decks tall, with a roof and a door in the side,

'cos I'm gon-na make it rain and rain and rain and

8

No. 2

12

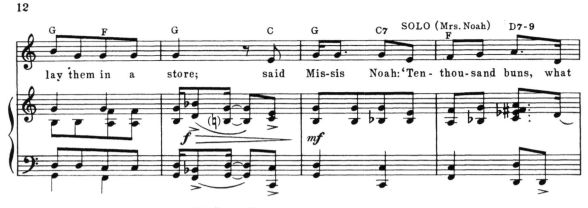

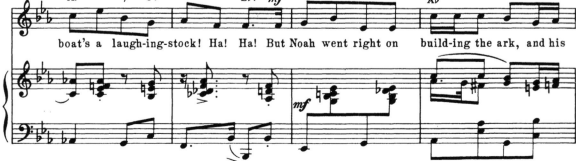

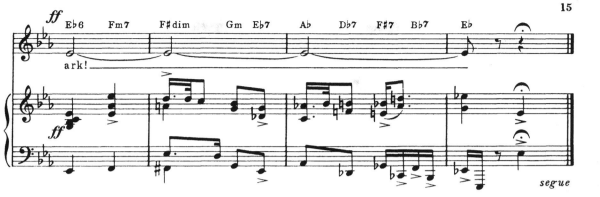

No. 3

All mar-su-pi-als and mam-mals, such as wal-la-bies and cam-els, snakes and cen-ti-pedes, a pair of ev-'ry one; they got stuck with one gir - affe, till they found his bet-ter half, then from an-te-lope to ze-bra, it was done! Yes,

'Noah! Noah! Don't do a-ny more!' said the

peo-ple, 'what a lark!' As crea-tures

came by ev-'ry name, and he led them in-to the ark, No-ah!

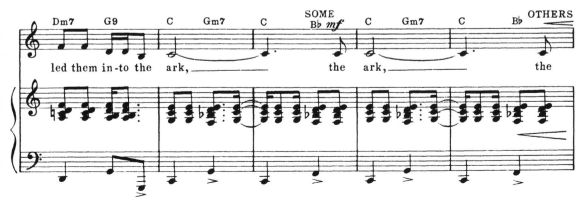

led them in-to the ark, _____ the ark, _____ the

ark! _____ With

Mis - sis Shem and Mis - sis Ham and_ Mis - sis Ja - phet too, and

Mis - sis Noah and their hus - bands four, they went in two by two. 'Is

ev -'ry liv - ing crea - ture there, be - fore I shut the door? Are you

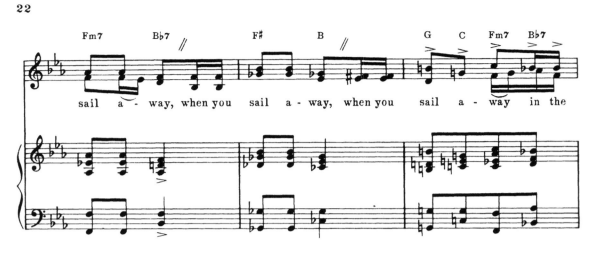

sail a - way, when you sail a - way, when you sail a - way in the

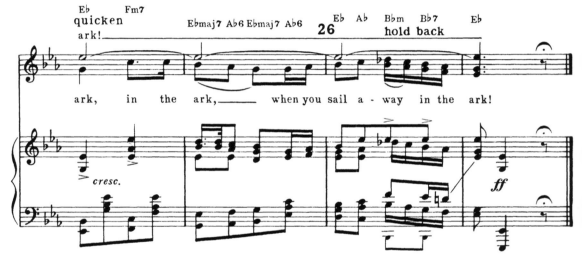

ark, in the ark, when you sail a - way in the ark!

No. 4

27

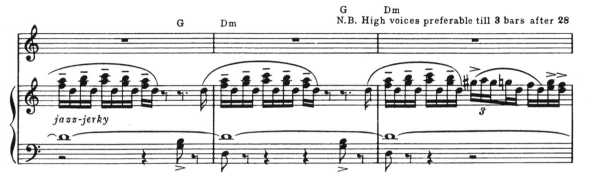

N.B. High voices preferable till **3** bars after **28**

jazz-jerky

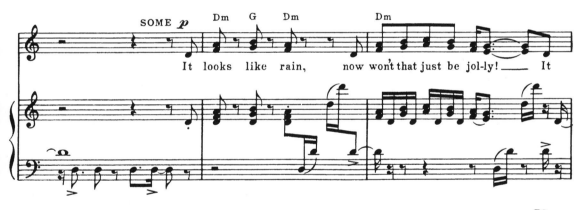

It looks like rain, now won't that just be jol-ly!___ It

looks like rain, you know, I thought it would! It

marcato

19888

looks like rain, I must go and get my brol-ly; a short, sharp show-er will

do the flow-ers good!

It

looks like rain— in fact, it's real-ly

26

please!   Oh God   for - give   me

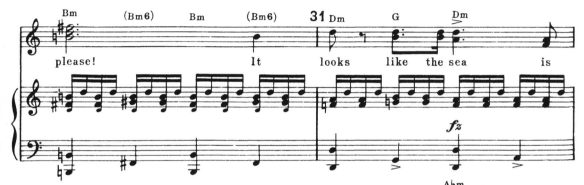

please!   It   looks   like   the   sea   is

ri - sing like a foun - tain; it   looks   like... HELP!   I'm

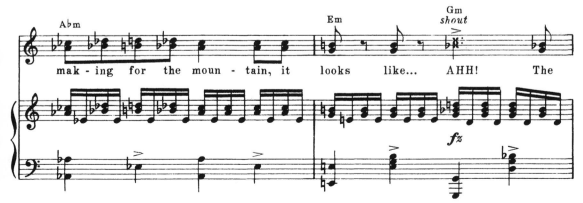

mak - ing for the moun - tain, it looks like... AHH!   The

worlds a brim-ming jug! The wa-ter's round my shoul-ders and I'm Glug! Glug!

slower ♩ = 84

Glug!

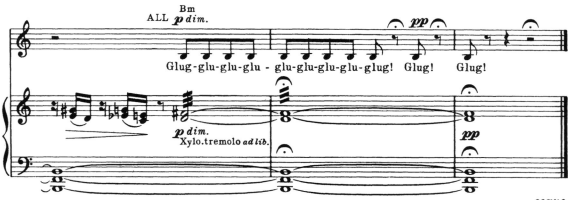

ALL

Glug - glu - glu - glu - glu - glu - glu - glu - glug! Glug! Glug!

Xylo. tremolo ad lib.

segue

No. 5

earth did drown; ____ for ev-en the peaks of the moun -

tains were a good five fath-oms down, way down, a good five

fath-oms down. ____ But the

Lord he re-mem-bered his pro-mise ____ and the ark went float-ing free, ____

No. 6

as it sailed on the end-less sea.

For-ty days and nights liv-ing un-der hatch-es. Care-ful with the lights! Feed the beasts in batch-es! And I can't hear them roar as they're

no more oil for burn-ing, and I just can't breathe, and my feet are made of

lead! And the rain's stead-y drum-ming on the roof a-bove my head, the

rain-drops drum-ming o-ver-head! For-ty days at

sea, how the tim-bers shud-der! God has pro-mised

35

19888

head! The rain's stopped drum-ming o - ver - head!

rain's stopped drum-ming o - ver - head! drum-ming o - ver - head!

segue

No. 7

Mod. slow (but move) ♩ = 96

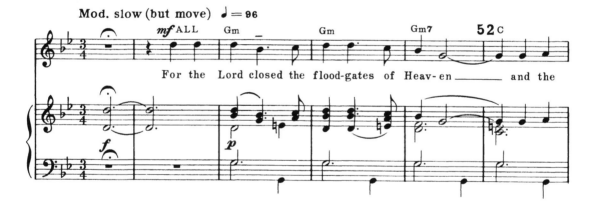

For the Lord closed the flood-gates of Heav- en _____ and the

springs of the deep blue sea, _____ and he sent a west wind blow-ing ____

38

to dry it up grad-ual-ly._____ The wa-ters slow-ly sub-

sid-ed_____ o-ver ma-ny long days and weeks_____ till one

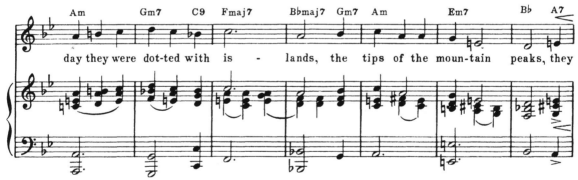

day they were dot-ted with is - lands, the tips of the moun-tain peaks, they

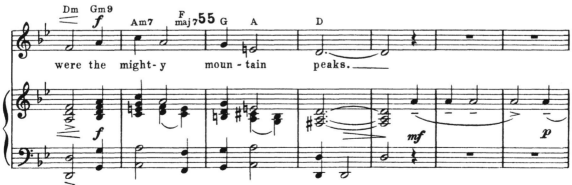

were the might-y moun-tain peaks._____

The ark went peace-ful-ly float - ing___ and the sea was

calm and flat_____ till the Lord_ God brought it to rest at

last, on the top of Mount A - ra - rat,_____ on top of Mount

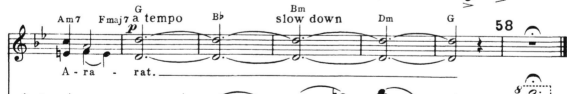

A - ra - rat.___

No. 8

Fa-ther Noah please o - pen the port-hole,

let's have a peep at the world out - side; though we thank the Lord who saved us —

Cain and A - bel! What a ride! Can't be-lieve the ark's not mo-ving,

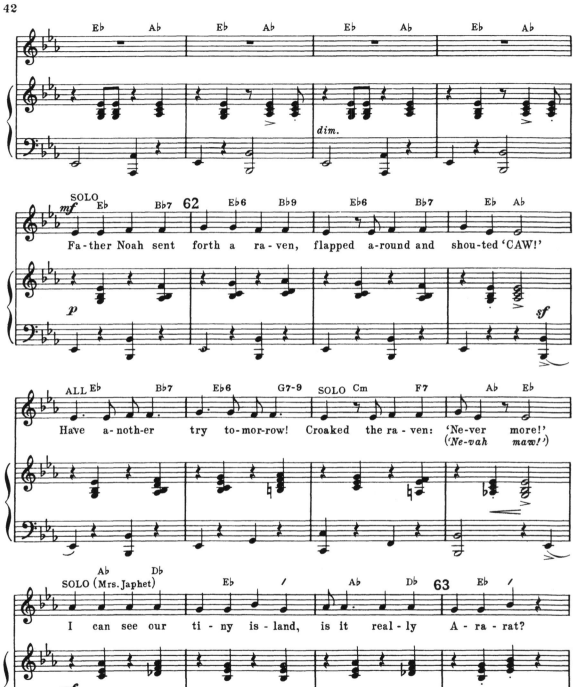

Fa - ther Noah sent forth a ra - ven, flapped a - round and shou - ted 'CAW!'

Have a - noth - er try to - mor - row! Croaked the ra - ven: 'Ne - ver more!'
('Ne - vah maw!')

SOLO (Mrs. Japhet)

I can see our ti - ny is - land, is it real - ly A - ra - rat?

Let me lean out e - ven fur-ther... There goes Mis - sis Ja-phet's hat!

Let's have a peep through the port - hole, Fa - ther! Mis - sis Ham must

have a shot! So you boys can see my bloo - mers?

Thank you, No! I'd ra - ther not!

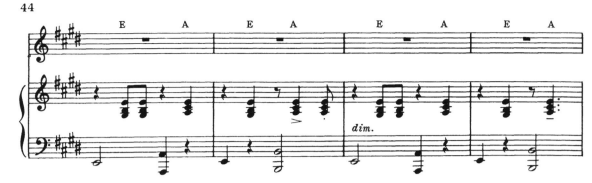

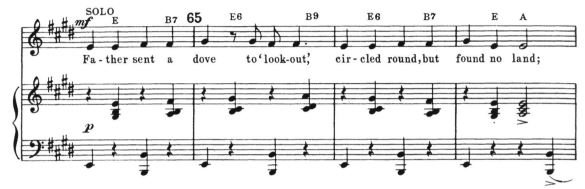

Fa - ther sent a dove to 'look-out,' cir - cled round, but found no land;

then it flew right back through the port-hole, set-tled safe on Fa-ther's hand.

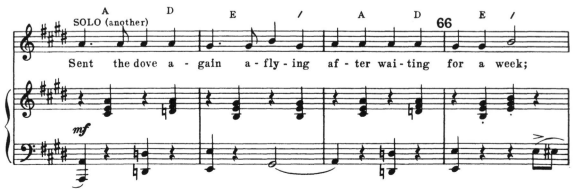

Sent the dove a - gain a - fly - ing af - ter wai - ting for a week;

steadier

SOLO

One more week, then off we sent it, wai-ted all that day, and then

sent the oth-er dove to join it; nei-ther one came back a-gain!

MORE VOICES

Now they need no ark for shel-ter, there the doves will build their nest—

hold back

where the o-live trees are grow-ing make their home and take their rest.

No. 9

49

there and set the a-ni-mals free and the birds of the air,' and they came out two by two by two by two by two; (run-ning down the gang-plank!) two by two by two by two by two. The Lord said: 'Go where it suits you best, and

72A

co-ver the earth from East to West, by two by two by two by two by

two.' They came out two. But

not slower, but more serious

dog and cat and ox and ass I give for Noah to keep, with chick-en, tur-key, duck and goose and

horse and goat and sheep. And Man shall sow and till the ground, and fill it with in-crease, while

No. 10

This is my pro-mise to you,_____ the rain-bow o-ver-

head:_____ vi - o-let, in-di-go, blue and green,

all the co-lours that lie be - tween vi - o-let, in-di-go,

blue_ and green, yel - low, o-range and red!_____

CANTATAS IN POPULAR STYLE

BLYTON, Carey
DRACULA!
A Victorian melodrama for narrator, unison voices and piano, based on Bram Stoker's book
[Duration 30 minutes]

FRANKENSTEIN!
A Victorian melodrama for narrator, unison voices and piano, based on Mary Shelley's book
[Duration 40 minutes]

SWEENEY TODD THE BARBER
A Victorian melodrama for narrator, unison voices and piano
[Duration 17 minutes]

CHAPPELL, Herbert
THE DANIEL JAZZ
Unison voices and piano
[Duration 10 minutes]

HAZELL, Chris
HOLY MOSES
Unison voices and piano with optional bass and drums
[Duration 22 minutes]

HOROVITZ, Joseph & FLANDERS, Michael
CAPTAIN NOAH & HIS FLOATING ZOO
Unison or two part voices and piano with optional bass and drums
[Duration 26 minutes]

HURD, Michael
ADAM-IN-EDEN
The story of Adam and Eve and that snake in the grass for unison voices (with divisions) and piano, with guitar chord symbols
[Duration 21 minutes]

CAPTAIN CORAM'S KIDS
An 'eighteenth-century pop cantata' for narrator, unison voices and piano
[Duration 19 minutes]

HIP-HIP HORATIO
A mock 'oratorio' for narrator (tenor), chorus (high and low voices) and piano
[Duration 30 minutes]

JONAH-MAN JAZZ
Unison voices and piano
[Duration 10 minutes]

THE LIBERTY TREE
A 'ballad cantata' for narrator, unison voices and piano
[Duration 30 minutes]

A NEW NOWELL
A Christmas cantata for unison voices (with divisions) and piano
[Duration 19 minutes]

PILGRIM
A musical morality, based on 'Pilgrim's Progress', for narrator, unison voices (with divisions) and piano (guitar chord symbols are included in the vocal score)
[Duration 18 minutes]

ROOSTER RAG
For narrator, unison voices, with optional divisions and piano (guitar chord symbols are included in the vocal score)
[Duration 13 minutes]

SWINGIN' SAMSON
For narrator, unison voices and divisions and piano
[Duration 10 minutes]

LLOYD WEBBER, Andrew & RICE, Tim
JOSEPH AND THE AMAZING TECHNICOLOUR DREAMCOAT
Unison voices and piano.
[Complete version duration 60 minutes, abridged version duration 20 minutes]

Approval copies sent on request